AFRICAN ANIMALS
Pythons

by Jody Sullivan Rake
Consulting Editor: Gail Saunders-Smith, PhD

Consultant:
George Wittemyer, PhD
NSF International Postdoctoral Fellow
University of California at Berkeley

Capstone
press®

Mankato, Minnesota

Pebble Plus is published by Capstone Press,
151 Good Counsel Drive, P.O. Box 669, Mankato, Minnesota 56002.
www.capstonepress.com

1 2 3 4 5 6 13 12 11 10 09 08

Library of Congress Cataloging-in-Publication Data
Rake, Jody Sullivan
    Pythons / by Jody Sullivan Rake.
    p. cm. — (Pebble plus. African animals)
    Includes bibliographical references and index.
    ISBN-13: 978-1-4296-1250-0 (hardcover)
    ISBN-10: 1-4296-1250-9 (hardcover)
    1. Pythons — Juvenile literature. I. Title. II. Series.
QL666.O67R35 2008
597.96'78096 — dc22   2007028680

Summary: Discusses pythons, their African habitat, food, and behavior.

Editorial Credits
Erika L. Shores, editor; Renée T. Doyle, designer, Laura Manthe, photo researcher

Photo Credits
BigStockPhoto.com/Belinda de Sousa, 22
Bruce Coleman Inc./John Giustina, 16–17
Corbis/Paul A. Souders, 4–5
Dreamstime/Ankevanwyk, 10–11
fotolia/Marti Timple, 6–7
The Image Finders/Fritz Polking, 14–15
iStockphoto/Nathan Menifee, 1
Jupiter Images, 20–21
Peter Arnold/Gunter Ziesler, 12–13
Shutterstock/Lucian Coman, 8–9; Ozger Aybike Sarikaya, cover, 1, 3 (snake skin); Thomas Bedenk, cover
SuperStock/ZSSD, 18–19

Note to Parents and Teachers

The African Animals set supports national science standards related to life science.
This book describes and illustrates pythons. The images support early readers in
understanding the text. The repetition of words and phrases helps early readers learn
new words. This book also introduces early readers to subject-specific vocabulary words,
which are defined in the Glossary section. Early readers may need assistance to read
some words and to use the Table of Contents, Glossary, Read More, Internet Sites, and
Index sections of the book.

Table of Contents

Living in Africa

Pythons live in Africa.

These big snakes like living

in warm, wet places.

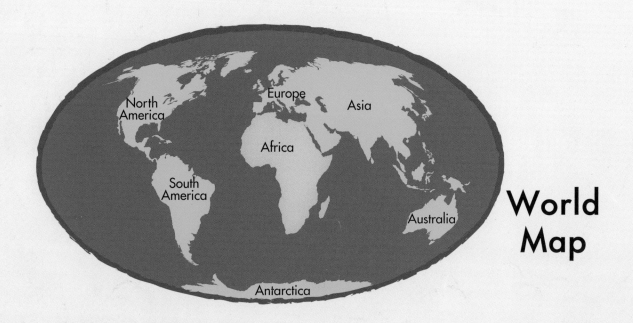

World Map

Some pythons climb
forest trees.
Other pythons slither
through grasslands.

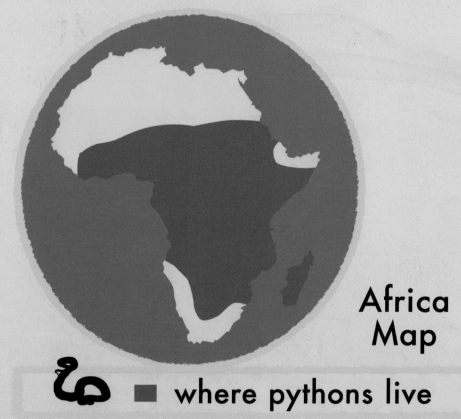

Africa
Map

🐍 ■ where pythons live

6

Up Close!

Pythons are long.

Some pythons are
longer than two cars.

9

Pythons are covered with
smooth, shiny scales.
Pythons shed their scaly skin
as they grow.

Eating

Pythons hunt antelope, monkeys, and crocodiles. Pythons wrap their bodies around prey and squeeze it to death.

Pythons open their jaws wide
to swallow prey whole.
A python can wait a year
between meals if its prey
is very large.

Staying Safe

Predators don't attack
adult pythons.
But eggs and small pythons
are tasty treats
to hungry crocodiles.

A female python hides
her eggs from predators.
She wraps her body around
the eggs to keep them safe.

The female python
does not care for
her young after they hatch.
Be careful, little pythons!

Glossary

grassland — a large, open area where grass and low plants grow

hatch — to break out of an egg

hunt — to find and kill animals for food

predator — an animal that hunts other animals for food

prey — an animal that is hunted by another animal

scale — a small, hard plate that covers the body of a snake

shed — to let something fall off or drop off

squeeze — to press something firmly; pythons squeeze their prey until it cannot breathe.

Read More

Fiedler, Julie. *Pythons.* Scary Snakes. New York: PowerKids Press, 2008.

Murray, Julie. *Pythons.* A Buddy Book. Animal Kingdom. Edina, Minn.: Abdo, 2003.

Weber, Valerie J. *African Rock Pythons.* World's Largest Snakes. Milwaukee: Gareth Stevens, 2003.

Internet Sites

FactHound offers a safe, fun way to find Internet sites related to this book. All of the sites on FactHound have been researched by our staff.

Here's how:

1. Visit *www.facthound.com*

2. Choose your grade level.

3. Type in this book ID **1429612509** for age-appropriate sites. You may also browse subjects by clicking on letters, or by clicking on pictures and words.

4. Click on the **Fetch It** button.

FactHound will fetch the best sites for you!

Index

Word Count: 139
Grade: 1
Early-Intervention Level: 16